LANGUAGE LESSONS

FOR TODAY

GRADE 4

MY FATHER'S
WORLD®

Language Lessons for Today is adapted from **Intermediate Language Lessons** by Emma Serl, American Book Company, 1914, as well as portions of *Primary Lessons in Language and Composition* by William Maxwell, American Book Company, 1886; *First Book in English* by William Maxwell, American Book Company, 1894; and *Language Lessons* by Lawton Evans, American Book Company, 1908, with significant revisions, updated language and examples, and additional new content.

Published by
My Father's World®
PO Box 2140, Rolla, MO 65402
(573) 202-2000
www.mfwbooks.com
November 2022

Contents

ANSWER KEY

Most of the lessons in this book do not require an answer key. The Answer Key for lessons that require it is available online at mfwbooks.com/LLTAnswers (free download; login required) or in the *Answer Key Language Lessons for Today* available separately from My Father's World.

Introduction

Language Lessons for Today follows the Charlotte Mason method of language arts instruction that encourages children to explore and expand upon the language that they already know. Learning to use language better to communicate with others becomes the reason for study, rather than analyzing language for purely academic reasons. We believe a study of language arts must go beyond grammar, mechanics, usage, and spelling. These are servants that lead to a higher goal—the art of communication: speaking, listening, reading, and writing.

Through short, interactive, teacher-led lessons, *Language Lessons for Today* gives children an opportunity to improve their speaking, listening, reading, and writing skills. Their powers of observation and elocution are enhanced through simple picture study and conversation lessons. Their exposure to fine examples of our language by hearing short stories and poems read aloud and by memorizing or retelling those increases their understanding of sentence structure and improves their vocabulary. Copying a passage introduces them to the rules of mechanics, grammar, and spelling in a gentle and natural way. An introduction to the function of words in earlier years provides a foundation for the study of the parts of speech in later years.

Informal language arts lessons for vocabulary, composition, listening comprehension, and handwriting are found in the history, science, and Bible activities in My Father's World curriculum. *Language Lessons for Today* is a resource that fits well with My Father's World curriculum; add spelling for a well-rounded language arts program.

This book is designed to be non-consumable to keep the cost lower as books may be reused. Even more important, this format encourages oral (instead of written) lessons. Children love the one-on-one time with parents/teachers. Oral lessons allow the adult to give immediate feedback on errors, focus on the student's needs, and modify the lesson (or add more explanation) when needed. Consumable workbooks tend to be done independently without immediate feedback if an error is made. Oral lessons can also focus on specific language concepts without the stress of writing. For many students, the labor of handwriting keeps them from learning the actual concept you are trying to teach!

The short, focused lessons generally take about 15 minutes to complete. Plan to complete three lessons a week. Simply open the book and read the lesson to the children. They will answer many of the questions orally. When written responses are required, use notebook paper and file the sheets in a 3-ring binder. Younger children may find it easier to write on every other line when using notebook paper.

The lessons may be used exactly as written or adapted for a child's specific needs and learning style. Many of the lessons that seem to require written work are easy to adapt so that a child simply answers orally. This is especially important with a younger child who finds writing too laborious. Also, you may increase *or* decrease the amount of written work in lessons based on how much writing the child is doing in other subjects that day.

Some lessons have directions such as "Fill the blanks" or "Tell..." which allow the option of written or oral answers. Lessons that are specific with directions such as "Write..." should generally be completed as written, but this is at the teacher's discretion.

Preface from Original 1914 Edition of Intermediate Language Lessons *(excerpt)*

The purpose of this book is to aid pupils to speak and write the English language correctly.

Attention is called to the following features: Literature studies, not only in poetry, but also in fine prose selections. Letter writing on subjects that appeal to child life. Drill on correct forms of speech and words often misused. Many exercises to increase the pupil's vocabulary. The various forms in composition, including description, narration, conversation, and dialogue. Both reproduction and original work in oral and written composition. Sequence and careful gradation in arrangement of lessons. The careful treatment of capitalization and punctuation. Observation lessons which furnish material for talking and writing.

The oral composition in connection with the observation lessons not only aid the pupil in telling readily and accurately what he has seen, but give him self-possession and train him to logical thought.

When an essential fact is taught, the pupil is given practice in using the fact again and again, through dictation, reproduction, and original composition.

Explanation of Lesson Types

You will encounter a variety of lessons in *Language Lessons for Today*, some of which may be new to you and are described below:

Oral Composition (*See Lesson 2*) — These lessons can look simple, but we encourage you not to skip any. Oral composition lessons help develop the thought process needed later for written composition. If students give one- or two-word answers, you can provide good models by answering similar questions with complete sentences.

Picture Study (*See Lesson 5*) — One of the purposes of picture study is to increase the power of observation. Many of the pictures in this book are copies of the works of great artists. You read the questions, and the children answer by looking carefully at the picture. Prompt them to use complete sentences when answering. A few suggestive questions are given with each picture. You may supplement these with a few questions of your own.

Poem to Memorize (*See Lesson 7*) — Poetry memorization helps children internalize excellent models of the English language. A child who memorizes vocabulary words and sentence structure in poems will more easily use those words and structures in daily conversation.

We encourage you to help your students memorize some of the poems in this book. (You may choose just the first part of the poem if it seems too long.) When the book requires a poem to be memorized, spread that work out for the whole week. Students do not need to memorize all the poems in the book, but we do encourage you to stretch their abilities and expect some memorization. All of these selections should be read aloud to the students and discussed whether they are memorized or not. Children can often memorize much more than we think if we approach the task positively and give support and encouragement. Our children enjoyed the reward of calling Grandma and reciting the memorized poem or stanza.

Some children memorize poems easily and quickly and need minimal adult assistance. However, many children will need more adult guidance. You might post the poem on a wall or the refrigerator, and read the poem together once or twice daily for a week.

Copywork (*See Lesson 8*) — The purpose of copywork is to familiarize students with spelling, mechanics, and usage while practicing handwriting. Have them copy part or all of the selection on appropriate handwriting or notebook paper. If you find the copywork too long in a lesson, then assign just a part of it, or allow more than one day to complete it.

Dictation (*See Lesson 11*) — Let students look at the book as you discuss the more difficult words and the punctuation. Point out difficult words to spell and practice them. Then remove the book, and slowly read the sentence aloud. Have the students repeat the sentence aloud and then write it. You may break up the sentence into smaller phrases if needed.

Poem to Read Aloud (*See Lesson 16*) — These poems are to read aloud to the students. They are not memorized but simply enjoyed.

Oral Narration (*See Lesson 31*) — The children simply listen to you read the story aloud, and then let one or more retell it. Before you begin, remind the children to listen carefully and be ready to tell the story in their own words when you are finished reading. Don't worry if a child gives an incomplete narration. If your children are new to narration, you may ask a few guided questions to help them remember the basic plot of the story. Narration takes practice and will improve over time.

Dictionary Usage is introduced beginning in Lesson 10. We recommend *Merriam-Webster's Elementary Dictionary*, which is available from My Father's World.

Lesson 1
Selection for Study—The Stone in the Road

Read the story aloud.

There was once a king who lived in a beautiful palace near a little village. He loved the people in the village and tried in many ways to help them.

But the people were selfish and did not try to help one another. The good king wished to teach them a lesson, so he arose early one morning and placed a large stone in the road which led past his palace. Then, hiding himself nearby, he watched to see what would happen.

Soon a woman came along driving some goats to pasture. She grumbled because the stone was in the way, and stepping over it, she went on up the road.

By and by a man came riding a donkey. He complained about the stone but drove around it and went on his way.

Other people came and went. Each remarked about the stone, but no one tried to move it.

At last, when the day was almost ended, the miller's boy came down the road. Seeing the stone, he halted and put down the bundle he was carrying.

"This stone should not be here," he said. "Someone might fall over it. I will move it out of the way."

The stone was heavy, and the boy could scarcely lift it. But by repeated efforts he at last pushed it from its place and rolled it to one side. As he turned to continue on his way, he saw something where the stone had been. There was a bag with writing on it. Bending closer he read these words: "This bag of gold belongs to the one who helps others by removing the stone from the road."

The miller's boy carried his treasure home with a happy heart. The king returned to his palace, saying, "I am glad I found someone unselfish enough to think of others."

Tell the story using the following points. You can look at this list as you retell the story.

> king puts stone in road
> people pass by
> miller's boy moves stone
> miller's boy rewarded

Look at the last paragraph of the story. Tell where and why these are used: period, comma, quotation marks.

With what kind of letter is the word *I* always written? Make a rule for this use of the capital letter.

Lesson 2
Oral Composition—The Hidden Jewel

> » *Teacher: Before teaching today's lesson, read the information about Oral Composition on page 8.*

Read the story, "The Stone in the Road." Then make a similar story about a king and a beautiful jewel. The king places the jewel in a bucket far down in a deep well, and then he disguises himself as a poor man. He asks all who pass to draw water for him to drink.

Begin your story this way: Once upon a time, a king ———.

Make a list of the three to five main points in your story.

Tell your story, using your list.

Lesson 3
Declarative Sentences and Interrogative Sentences

A **sentence** is a group of words that expresses a complete thought. With what kind of letter does a sentence begin?

1. A king lived in a beautiful palace.
2. Where did he hide the gold?
3. What would you do with a bag of gold?
4. The unselfish boy was rewarded.

Which of the above sentences tell something? A sentence that tells (or declares) something is a **declarative sentence**. What mark of punctuation is placed after a declarative sentence?

Which of the above sentences ask something? A sentence that asks (or interrogates) about something is an **interrogative sentence**. What mark of punctuation is placed after an interrogative sentence?

Write three declarative sentences about the picture in Lesson 5. Next to each one, write "declarative." Then write three interrogative sentences about the picture. Next to each one, write "interrogative."

Lesson 4
Imperative Sentences and Exclamatory Sentences

Do you know the four kinds of sentences?

Declarative Sentence – statement
Interrogative Sentence – question
Imperative Sentence – command
Exclamatory Sentence – exclamation

Read the following sentences:

1. I just ripped my shirt!
2. That spider is huge!
3. Please be seated.
4. Try again.

Which of the above sentences command or request something? A sentence that commands or requests something is an **imperative sentence**. What mark of punctuation is placed after an imperative sentence?

Which of the above sentences show excitement and strong feeling? A sentence that shows excitement or strong feeling is an **exclamatory sentence**. What mark of punctuation is placed after an exclamatory sentence?

Say two imperative sentences. Then say two exclamatory sentences.

Write four kinds of sentences about a puppy or your pet: declarative, interrogative, imperative, and exclamatory. Label each one to tell which kind of sentence it is.

Lesson 5
Picture Study—Noah's Ark

> » *Teacher: Before teaching today's lesson, read the information about Picture Study on page 8.*

In the painting *Noah's Ark*, the animals are not wildly running or panicked; they are peaceful. Two by two they wait in a line, patiently waiting their turn to enter the ark that invites any that will come to be saved from the storm. Edward Hicks's paintings are invitations to the peace of Christ.

Contrast means to see the differences. Contrast what you see in the upper part of the painting to the lower part. Contrast any other items in the painting.

Why do you think Mr. Hicks had the lion and lamb standing near one another? Why is this unexpected, or ironic? What is in the center of the painting? Why do you think this is an important part of the painting?

Many different types of lines are used in this picture. Point to curved lines. Point to horizontal lines. Point to slanted lines. (The slanted line on the entrance to the ark helps emphasize its importance.)

Find and name as many different types of shapes as you can.

What message is Mr. Hicks giving through his painting?

> » *Teacher: See answers for today's lesson on page 4-2 of the* Answer Key *(available in print or online; see page 5).*

Imagine being a thirteen-year-old living in Pennsylvania in 1793. No cars zoom down the road. Instead, horses pull carriages. Imagine you are painting a new carriage. You carefully write the letters that spell the name of the company buying the coach. Then you decorate the coach, painting

Edward Hicks

NOAH'S ARK

with care. For seven years, Edward Hicks did just this, learning to be an expert coach and sign painter.

From this experience, Edward found he was gifted as an artist. He gave his gift to God and was inspired to paint more than sixty paintings depicting the Peaceable Kingdom, showing that different people can live and work together peacefully. Edward Hicks painted George Washington crossing the Delaware River on Christmas Eve, William Penn and the Pennsylvania settlers having a peaceable meeting with Native Americans, and various children and "wild" animals living peacefully with one another.

Optional drawing assignment: Can you see the way Mr. Hicks made the animals look three-dimensional as though many of them are stepping forward? Do you see the arches in some of their backs? Can you imagine the muscles in their bodies? Do you see circular and wavy lines he painted to depict these muscles? Select one animal and draw or paint it by using different types of shapes and lines, especially wavy and slanted lines. Try to reveal the animal's muscles. Are the tree trunks straight sticks, or do they have curvy lines? Draw one of the trees you see in the picture.

Lesson 6
Oral Composition

Tell a story that one of the animals in the picture *Noah's Ark* might tell another animal.

Begin it this way:

> This morning when I woke up I ——.

Lesson 7
Poem to Memorize

> » *Teacher: Before teaching today's lesson, read the information about Poem to Memorize on page 8.*

True Worth

True worth is in being, not seeming;
    In doing each day that goes by
Some little good; not in the dreaming
    Of great things to do by and by.
For whatever men say in their blindness,
    And spite of the fancies of youth,
There's nothing so kingly as kindness,
    And nothing so royal as truth.

—ALICE CARY

Talk about the meaning of this poem.

Begin to memorize and copy "True Worth."
How many lines are indented? Where will you need to use capital letters?

Lesson 8
Copywork

> » *Teacher: Before teaching today's lesson, read the information about Copywork on page 9.*

Finish memorizing and copying the poem "True Worth."

Optional: Draw an illustration for the poem.

Lesson 9
The Subject of a Sentence

1. A bird flies.
2. Airplanes fly.
3. Squirrels leap.
4. Babies crawl.

What is the person or thing in the first sentence?

What is the person or thing in the second sentence?

What is the person or thing in the third sentence?

What is the person or thing in the fourth sentence?

The person or thing discussed is called the **subject**.

What is the subject of the first sentence? the second? the third? the fourth?

> The **subject** tells who or what the sentence is about.

Say the four sentences above, but change them so that you speak of only one thing in each sentence.

In the Woods

____ bloom. ____ sing. ____ buzz. ____ play. ____ rustle.
____ ripen.

Copy this paragraph. Fill the blanks with suitable subjects, one word for each. Underline the subject in each sentence.

Lesson 10
The Dictionary

» *Teacher: You will need a dictionary to teach some of the lessons this year.*

How are words in the dictionary arranged?

How is the pronunciation of a word indicated? Find the pronunciation key in your dictionary. Look at the symbols that are used and read aloud the sample words.

Find the following words in your dictionary. Copy each word, dividing it into syllables. Then copy the pronunciation as given in the dictionary. Pronounce the words.

1. compassion
2. scroll
3. flax
4. pyramid
5. dynasty

Lesson 11
Subject Review and Composition

» *Teacher: Before teaching today's lesson, read the information about Dictation on page 9.*

Two goats walked on a narrow bridge.
The goats met at the middle of the bridge.
The goats fought for the right of way.
The two goats fell into the water.

What is the subject of the first sentence? (Remember, the subject tells who or what the sentence is about.) What is the subject of the second sentence? the third sentence? the fourth sentence?

The four sentences at the top of the page tell a story. Do you think the story runs along smoothly? Is it very interesting?

Read the following story:

The Foolish Goats

One day a goat started out for a walk. He went along quietly until he came to a very narrow bridge. At the middle of this bridge, he met another goat. Then the trouble began.

Both goats must have been very stubborn. Neither goat would allow the other to pass. They butted each other and locked horns. Splash! Both fell into the water and were drowned.

Is this story more interesting? How is it different from the first story?

» *Teacher: See answers on page 4-2 of the* Answer Key.

Optional: Copy or write from dictation part of this story.

Lesson 12
Names (Nouns)

rainbow	Egypt
desk	heat
thunder	boy

Which of these words is the name of a place? of a piece of furniture? of a person?

Which word names something we know only through the sense of hearing? through the sense of touch? through the sense of sight?

These words are *nouns*.

> A **noun** names a person, place, or thing.

Say a sentence for each of these nouns:

kindness	Atlantic Ocean	owls
Frank	potatoes	music

Write a noun for each of the following:

1. A tool
2. A piece of clothing
3. A fruit
4. A part of the body
5. An occupation
6. A country (Use a capital letter.)
7. A city (Use a capital letter.)
8. A person's name (Use a capital letter.)

Lesson 13
Composition

Read the following story:

The Wolf in Sheep's Clothing

The wolf was hungry.
The wolf put on a sheepskin to hide.
The wolf went to the sheep.

The shepherd saw the wolf pretending to be a sheep.
The shepherd caught the wolf.
The shepherd saved the sheep.

Read the sentences above. What is the subject of each sentence?

Write the story of the wolf in sheep's clothing. You may write the story in two paragraphs. You can use parts of the sentences above, but be sure to make your story more interesting.

Finish your rough draft today.

Lesson 14
Composition

Read your composition from Lesson 13 aloud to your parent/teacher.

Then do one or more of the following:

Tell what could happen next in your story.
Illustrate your story.
Recopy your story neatly.
Edit and rewrite the story with help from your parent/teacher.

Lesson 15
Singular and Plural Nouns

picture	chair	year
pictures	chairs	years

All of these words are nouns. Which of these nouns mean only one thing? Those are *singular* nouns. Which mean more than one? Those are *plural* nouns. What letter was added to make the words plural?

A noun that names one person, place, or thing is **singular**.
A noun that names more than one person, place, or thing is **plural**.

Now read these words and tell if they are singular or plural.

church	brush	dress
churches	brushes	dresses

What is added to *church* to make it mean more than one? to *brush*? to *dress*?

Try to pronounce *churches* without the *e*. Why do we add *es* instead of *s* to *church*?

To form a plural noun:

Usually add *s*.

If it ends with *s*, *z*, *ch*, *sh*, or *x*, add *es*.

Write these sentences, changing the nouns so that they are plural. You will have to make small changes to other words, too, such as changing *sings* to *sing*.

1. The brown <u>thrush</u> sings.
2. The gold <u>watch</u> keeps time.
3. This <u>box</u> was broken.
4. The <u>glass</u> has been washed.
5. A <u>ditch</u> was dug.

   » *Teacher: See answers on page 4-2 of the* Answer Key.

Lesson 16
Poem to Read Aloud

» *Teacher: Before teaching today's lesson, read the information about Poem to Read Aloud on page 9.*

The Brown Thrush

There's a merry brown thrush sitting up in the tree;
He's singing to me! He's singing to me!
And what does he say, little girl, little boy?
"Oh, the world's running over with joy!
　　Don't you hear? Don't you see?
　　Hush! Look in my tree,
I'm as happy as happy can be!"

And the brown thrush keeps singing: "A nest, do you see,
And five eggs, hid by me in the juniper tree?
Don't meddle! don't touch! little girl, little boy,
Or the world will lose some of its joy!
　　Now I'm glad! Now I'm free!
　　And I always shall be,
If you never bring sorrow to me."

So the merry brown thrush sings away in the tree,
To you and to me, to you and to me;
And he sings all the day, little girl, little boy,
"Oh, the world's running over with joy;
　　But long it won't be,
　　Don't you know? Don't you see?
Unless we are as good as can be."

—Lucy Larcom

To whom is the thrush singing? What does he say in the first stanza?

What question does the thrush ask in the second stanza? What commands does he give? What exclamations does he make?

In the third stanza, what does the thrush say all the day? How should we act toward birds and their nests? toward other people?

Where are quotation marks used in the first stanza, and why? in the second stanza? in the third stanza?

Lesson 17
Copywork

Practice reading this story several times. Then read it aloud to your parent/ teacher. Explain the final sentence in your own words. Then carefully copy the final sentence using your best handwriting.

General Lee and the Bird

One day while General Lee was riding along a highway, he heard the faint cry of a little bird in distress on the ground by the side of the road. Dismounting, he took the little bird tenderly in his hands, and seeing that it had fallen out of its nest and was quite helpless, he placed it carefully again in the nest which was in the forks of a low tree.

A man does not lose any of his greatness by being kind to those in distress, even though it be to a helpless little bird.

Lesson 18
Oral Composition—Dogs

All dogs have similar characteristics, yet differ in other ways. Think about a Dalmatian and a poodle. Think about their appearance, size, intelligence, and uses. Look at the points below and talk about some **differences**. Contrast the Dalmatian and poodle by using words like *but*, *yet*, *however*, or *on the other hand*. (Example: The Dalmatian has ____; however, the poodle has ____.")

DALMATIAN	POODLE
spotted (white with black or brown spots)	solid (white, gray, apricot, or black)
straight fur that sheds	curly fur that doesn't shed
medium size	toy, miniature, medium, or standard size
first used in Dalmatia as guard dog to protect horses pulling wagons	first used as duck hunters in Germany

Now contrast a Dalmatian and a red fox using the following points.

<u>Dalmatian</u>	<u>Red Fox</u>
domestic animal (pet)	wild animal
born solid white but develops black or brown spots	born brown or gray; coat turns brown, golden, silver, or black
droopy ears	upright pointed ears
narrow, long, pointed tail that curves upward	long, bushy tail that hangs down

Lesson 19
Composition—Description

Write a paragraph describing the appearance of this book (or another book that is on your desk). Include the following:

   The title and subject
   The cover—material, color, design
   The paper—thick or thin
   The margins—narrow or wide
   The illustrations

Do not include any opinions. Only write facts—things you can observe about your book.

Lesson 20
Picture Study—The Wounded Companion

Describe the picture.

To which child do you think the dog belongs?
What is the artist's name?
What do you see lying on the ground?
Which boy would probably be a good veterinarian when he is older? Why do you think so?
Describe the children's clothing and guess what time in history this is.

Tell the story suggested by the picture.

» *Teacher: See answers on page 4-3 of the* Answer Key.

J. G. Brown

THE WOUNDED COMPANION

Lesson 21
Composition—Frisk and the Mirror

One day Frisk saw himself in the mirror. He thought he saw another dog. What do you think happened next?

Tell or write the story as if Frisk were telling it. Begin the story this way:

This morning, I went into the dining room. I was surprised to see another dog standing in front of me.

Lesson 22
Poem to Memorize

Some poetry is serious and thoughtful. Today's four selections are primarily for fun! Enjoy reading these poems aloud and select one to copy and memorize.

If

If all the land were apple pie,
And all the sea were ink;
And all the trees were bread and cheese,
What should we do for drink?

—ANONYMOUS

A Flea and a Fly in a Flue

A flea and a fly in a flue
Were imprisoned, so what could they do?
    Said the fly, "Let us flee,"
    Said the flea, "Let us fly,"
So they flew through a flaw in the flue.

—ANONYMOUS

The Man in the Wilderness

The man in the wilderness asked of me,
"How many strawberries grow in the sea?"
I answered him as I thought good,
"As many red herrings as grow in the wood."

—ANONYMOUS

As I Was Going to St. Ives

As I was going to St. Ives
I met a man with seven wives;
Every wife had seven sacks,
Every sack had seven cats,
Every cat had seven kits.
Kits, cats, sacks, and wives,
How many were going to St. Ives?

—ANONYMOUS

» *Teacher: See answer on page 4-3 of the* Answer Key.

Lesson 23
Copywork

Finish memorizing and copying one or more of the poems from Lesson 22.

Optional: Draw an illustration for the poem.

Lesson 24
Singular and Plural Nouns

When a noun ends in *y*, it can be a bit tricky to form the plural. Read these nouns:

lily   daisy
lilies   daisies

What is the last letter of *lily*? of *daisy*? How are these two words changed to make them plural?

Write (or spell aloud) the plural of these nouns:

baby	story
lady	cherry
berry	

Read these nouns. What do you notice about these plurals?

days	boys	chimneys

What letter is before *y* in *day*? in *boy*? in *chimney*? Are these consonants or vowels? How are these words changed to make them plural? When do we keep the *y*?

Notice that when a vowel is before *y*, we don't change the *y*. If a word ends in a vowel + *y*, we simply follow our usual rule—add *s*. So now our plural noun rule has three parts:

> To form a plural noun:
>
> Usually add *s*.
> If it ends with *s, z, ch, sh,* or *x*, add *es*.
> If it ends with a consonant + *y*,
> change *y* to *i*, and add *es*.

Change each of these nouns to plural and write questions using the plurals.

1. key
2. party
3. baby
4. monkey
5. berry
6. story

Lesson 25
Irregular Plural Nouns

Which of these words mean only one? Which are singular? Which of these words mean more than one? Which are plural?

man	child
men	children

The plurals of some nouns are formed in irregular ways. Read these nouns:

SINGULAR	PLURAL
mouse	mice
ox	oxen
goose	geese
foot	feet
man	men
woman	women
child	children
tooth	teeth
sheep	sheep
deer	deer
moose	moose
fish	fish

Write the following sentences, changing all the singular nouns to plural and all the plural nouns to singular. You will have to make other small changes so that the sentences sound (and are) correct. Review the rules in Lesson 24 before you begin.

Example:

The <u>butterfly</u> is orange.

Answer:

The butterflies are orange.

1. <u>Crows</u> annoy the <u>farmers</u>.
2. A <u>fox</u> caught his <u>tail</u> in the <u>trap</u>.
3. We gathered a <u>daisy</u>, a <u>lily</u>, and a <u>poppy</u>.
4. A <u>mouse</u>, an <u>ox</u>, and a <u>sheep</u> were in the <u>barn</u>.
5. The <u>story</u> was about a <u>boy</u>.

» *Teacher: See answers on page 4-3 of the* Answer Key.

Lesson 26
Action Words (Verbs)

Dolphins *swim*.
Birds *fly*.

Tell one thing you can do.

What are some of the things your mother does every day?

Tell one thing a horse can do. Tell another.

What noise does a dog make? a cat? a pig?

What do we do with our eyes? our ears? our noses? our mouths? our fingers?

All of these words are action words. Action words are also called **verbs**. Can you say five action words, or verbs?

Read these sentences. Can you say the verb in each one?

1. A bear growls.
2. A monkey chatters.
3. A cricket chirps.
4. A duck quacks.
5. A lion roars.

Can you say the noun in each sentence above?

Now write each of the sentences from above, but change it to talk about two animals. Begin like this:

1. Bears _____.

Lesson 27
Composition Skills (Sentence Combining)

Can you tell me three things birds do, using the word *birds* only once?
Can you tell me three things a boy does, using the word *boy* only once?

You might have said something like this:

Birds fly, sing, and make nests.
A boy rides his bike, plays soccer, and eats pizza.

Can you tell me the three action words, or verbs, in both of the sentences?
What punctuation marks are used in these sentences? Why?

» *Teacher: See answers on page 4-3 of the* Answer Key.

Combine each set of three statements into a single sentence. Use the word *and* only once in each sentence. Use correct punctuation.

1. Susan can sew.
   Susan can sing.
   Susan can play the piano.

2. John drew a picture.
   John wrote a story.
   John went outside to play.

3. The horse walks to the fence.
   The horse nudges my hand.
   The horse eats the grain.

4. The owl hoots.
   The owl sits in the tree.
   The owl looks wise.

Lesson 28
Poem to Read Aloud

Do you know who Lewis Carroll is? (By the way, *Lewis* and *Carroll* are special kinds of nouns, **proper nouns**, because they name a specific person. We'll talk more about proper nouns in a later lesson.)

Born in 1832 in England, Charles Lutwidge Dodgson (pen name Lewis Carroll) grew up in a family of seven sisters and three brothers. Though a shy boy who stammered, Charles excelled at creating games and had no trouble speaking to children. As an adult, he was a brilliant math teacher and math textbook writer. He is best known for his stories about an imaginative nonsense world and the character Alice, inspired by his friend Alice Liddell. His book, *Alice's Adventures in Wonderland*, is popular with children and adults alike. Even Queen Victoria adored it! That book includes a poem he wrote about a crocodile.

The Crocodile

How doth the little crocodile
Improve his shining tail,
And pour the waters of the Nile
On every golden scale!

How cheerfully he seems to grin!
How neatly spreads his claws,
And welcomes little fishes in
With gently smiling jaws!

—Lewis Carroll

If you used *Language Lessons for Today* Grade 3, you may remember a poem about a busy bee. Here are the first two stanzas. What do you notice when you compare the following poem to the poem "The Crocodile"?

Against Idleness and Mischief

How doth the little busy bee
Improve each shining hour,
And gather honey all the day
From every opening flower!

How skillfully she builds her cell!
How neat she spreads the wax!
And labors hard to store it well
With the sweet food she makes.

—Isaac Watts

Lesson 29
Possessive Nouns

Mary's book is on the table.

What mark and letter show that the book belongs to Mary? What do you call the mark? Spell aloud the word *apostrophe*. Where is an apostrophe placed? Where is letter *s* placed? An apostrophe and *s* tell us that someone owns, or possesses, something. A word like *Mary's* is called a ***possessive noun.***

What do these possessive nouns mean?

<u>Sally's</u> hat
the <u>rabbit's</u> ears
the <u>dog's</u> food

All of these possessive nouns tell us who owns something. Sally owns the hat, the ears belong to the rabbit, and the dog possesses the food.

Combine each of the following sets of statements into one sentence, each containing a possessive noun. Underline the possessive nouns.

Example:
The mill was burned.
It belonged to Mr. Simpson.

Answer:
Mr. Simpson's mill was burned.

1. Leslie owns a pony.
   It has long hair.
   It has shaggy hair.

2. Mrs. Walker owns a house.
   It is large.
   It is beautiful.
   It is purple.

3. The violin belongs to Mrs. Morrell.
   It is old.
   It is broken.

» *Teacher: See answers on page 4-4 of the* Answer Key.

Lesson 30
Composition—Dialogue

Mr. Robin and Mrs. Robin are trying to find a place for a nest. Mr. Robin wishes to build in the elm tree near the barn; Mrs. Robin says she is afraid of the cat. Mr. Robin suggests some other place, but Mrs. Robin does not like it. Mrs. Robin finds a branch in the maple tree that suits her. They begin to build the nest. Mrs. Robin brings some grass, and Mr. Robin finds a few pieces of string.

Write in dialogue form an imaginary conversation between the two. Give your dialogue a title. Notice that you do not use quotation marks in dialogues. Use this form:

MR. ROBIN: I really think it is time to build our nest.
MRS. ROBIN: _____
MR. ROBIN: _____

Lesson 31
Selection for Study—Oral Narration

» *Teacher: Before teaching today's lesson, read the information about Oral Narration on page 9.*

Read the story. Then tell it without looking at the book.

The Finding of Moses

Many hundreds of years ago in the land of Egypt, a Hebrew mother placed her baby boy in a basket made of bulrushes and hid him among the reeds by the riverside. She did this because Pharaoh, the king of the country, had ordered that all the Hebrew baby boys should be killed.

The mother left the child hidden there while his sister Miriam stood at a distance to watch.

Pharaoh's daughter went down to the Nile River to bathe. As she and her maids walked along the bank, they saw the basket among the rushes. Wondering what it could be, the princess asked one of her maids to bring it to her.

There in the basket of bulrushes, they found the baby boy. When he cried, the king's daughter had compassion on him and said, "This is one of the Hebrews' children."

Then his sister Miriam asked the princess, "Shall I go and call one of the Hebrew women, that she may nurse the baby for you?"

And the king's daughter said to her, "Go."

The sister ran quickly and got the baby's mother.

Pharaoh's daughter said to the mother, "Take the baby and nurse him for me, and I will pay you wages." So the mother took her own baby and nursed him.

When the child was older, he went to live with the king's daughter as her son. She called his name Moses, for she said, "I drew him out of the water."

Now summarize the story of baby Moses in four sentences. Look at the following phrases to help you organize your thoughts:

in basket
found
with mother
with Pharaoh's daughter

» *Teacher: You may need to complete this assignment first, modeling for the student how it is done. Then have the student attempt it. See an example on page 4-4 of the Answer Key.*

Lesson 32
Proper Nouns

In the story "The Finding of Moses," find:

the name of a country
the name of a river
the name of the baby
the name of the baby's sister

What kind of letter does the name of a person or country begin with?

All of the words you found are **nouns**, or name words. These nouns are called **proper nouns** because they name a specific person, place, or thing.

Say the names of

two countries
two famous people
two cities

All of the words you said are proper nouns. Proper nouns name a specific person, place, or thing. Tell me the proper noun in these sets:

boy — Jonathan
Nile River — river
state — Minnesota

Did you notice that both words in *Nile River* begin with a capital letter?

Tell me the rule for proper nouns and capital letters.

> Proper nouns begin with a capital letter. This includes names of people and places (such as cities, states, countries, bodies of water), days of the week, and months.

1. Write the names of three months.
2. Write the names of two days of the week.
3. Write the name of your state and its abbreviation. (State abbreviations use two capital letters and no period.)
4. Write the names of two vegetables. (Hint: These are not proper nouns.)
5. Write a sentence using four proper nouns. Underline the proper nouns.

Lesson 33
Picture Study—The Finding of Moses

Describe what you see in this picture.

How does the artist show that Moses, not Pharaoh's daughter, is most important in this picture? Who is everyone looking at? Do you see the two women extending their arms towards the baby?

How does Doré show which person is Pharaoh's daughter? Do you see how she is surrounded by those who care for her? She is wearing expensive clothes. Do you see the Egyptian headdresses and plush fans?

Now close your eyes and describe the picture in as much detail as you can.

Gustave Doré was a boy who loved to draw. When he was 15, he passed a shop window and saw engravings in the window that did not look quite right. Gustave went home and drew the pictures the way he thought they should look. He took his illustrations back to the store. The owner did not believe young Gustave had done the drawings, so he asked him to do more. The crowd was soon awed. Gustave was immediately offered a contract.

At age 15, Gustave Doré's first book, *The Labours of Hercules*, was published. The "Boy Genius" had written it, drawn illustrations for it, and engraved

Gustave Doré

THE FINDING OF MOSES

them in stone. Doré's work amazed people all over France where he became the highest paid illustrator in the country. "Cinderella," "Puss in Boots," "Sleeping Beauty," and Shakespeare's *Macbeth* are amongst the titles he illustrated. He produced 238 Bible engravings, 400 oil paintings, 1000 lithographs, and more than 10,000 engravings, making him the most popular illustrator of all time.

For most of Doré's life, the only way to illustrate a book was to do a wood engraving. Doré selected English Box tree wood so that he could do fine line carving without splinters. He looked for wood with evenly spaced rings so that the ink would penetrate equally, and for wood with a uniform color of yellow indicating equal hardness that allowed him to engrave uniform lines. With an iron hoop, he bound several pieces of wood together and sanded them. Next he set up a kerosene lamp. To protect his eyes, he donned a visor, and to prevent moisture in his breath from altering the wood, he put on a mask. Then he painted India ink on the wood. He drew a mirror image of his artwork so that when the final work was done, the viewer would see the print correctly. Next the wood would get a bath! That is, it would get a brick-bath with fine powder from ground bricks. Doré then gave each block to a different engraver. The workers used a graver tool to make outlines; a tint-tool to make parallel lines that would reveal tints, shades of gray, and shadows; and a gouger tool to remove large areas, which would leave white areas when the picture was printed. Finally the blocks were ready to print multiple copies of the illustration.

Lesson 34
Poem to Memorize

Out in the Fields with God

The little cares which fretted me,
I lost them yesterday
Among the fields, above the sea,
Among the winds at play;
Among the lowing of the herds,
The rustling of the trees,
Among the singing of the birds,
The humming of the bees.

The foolish fears of what might happen—
I cast them all away
Among the clover-scented grass,
Among the new-mown hay;
Among the husking of the corn,
Where drowsy poppies nod,
Where ill thoughts die and good are born—
Out in the fields with God.

—Elizabeth Barrett Browning

Can you find the word *fretted* in the poem?

Find *fret* or *fretted* in a dictionary. What are some words that might be used instead of *fretted*? Which do you like better, a word you found in the dictionary or the one the author uses?

The parts of a poem are called *stanzas*. How many stanzas are in this poem? With what kind of letter does the first word of each line of a poem begin?

1. What can you "hear" in the first stanza? What words does Browning use to help you hear these sounds? (Words that sound like the actual sound that is made are termed *onomatopoeia*.)
2. What can you "see" and "smell" in the second stanza?
3. What do you think the author is trying to tell us in this poem?

» *Teacher: See answers on page 4-4 of the* Answer Key.

Trotting her pony through the lush fields of England was one of Elizabeth Barrett Browning's most loved activities as a child in the early 1800s. Elizabeth, or "Ba" for short, lived on her father's farm, 500 acres of land which he bought when he sold Jamaican sugar plantations he had inherited. Elizabeth loved spending time with her father, Edward Barrett, and often said life was no fun without him. At age six she wrote her first poem, and by age fourteen her father had published her epic poem called *The Battle of Marathon*. Elizabeth was the oldest of twelve children, who enjoyed performing plays for their mother and father. Primarily educated at home, she read advanced books and poems by William Shakespeare, John Milton, and others before she was ten. She also learned Latin and could read the Old Testament in Hebrew. Elizabeth moved to Italy after she married Robert Browning, who was also a famous poet.

Begin to memorize and copy "Out in the Fields with God."

Lesson 35
Copywork

Finish memorizing and copying "Out in the Fields with God."

Optional: Draw an illustration for the poem.

Lesson 36
More About Possessive Nouns

What do you call more than one cat? What letter did you add?

Do you remember what *plural* means? The word *cats* is plural because there is more than one cat.

> The cats love milk.
> The cats' bowls are empty.

What is the difference between *cats* and *cats'* in the sentences above? What is the mark at the end of *cats'* called? You can look at Lesson 29 for help.

When a plural noun ends in *s*, add an apostrophe after the *s* to make it possessive.

Read these phrases. Say if the underlined noun is singular or plural and explain why the apostrophe is placed before or after the *s*.

1. <u>boys'</u> voices
2. <u>girl's</u> hair
3. <u>lions'</u> dens
4. <u>butterfly's</u> wings

Write sentences making these nouns possessive.

1. tigers
2. tree
3. table
4. Sam
5. rabbits
6. pony
7. ladies

» *Teacher: See answers on page 4-4 of the* Answer Key.

Lesson 37
Titles and Abbreviations

President Adams   Admiral Evans
Doctor Johnson   Judge Fuller
Uncle George   Pastor Jensen

All of these names include the person's title.

With what kind of letter does a person's title begin?
Tell me a rule for this use of the capital letter.

Words are sometimes written in a shorter way; they are then said to be *abbreviated*. Here are some common abbreviations. What punctuation mark follows an abbreviation?

Dr. – Doctor
Ave. – Avenue
Mr. – Mister
Mrs. – Missus (married woman)

Write one sentence using all four of the abbreviations listed above.

Lesson 38
The Comma in Direct Address

Mr. Brown, may we play baseball in your vacant lot?

Yes, Harry, you may if you won't be too noisy.

May I play after school, Mother?

A direct address is used when we speak directly to someone and say his or her name.

Who is addressed in the first sentence? What punctuation mark is placed after his name?

Who is addressed in the second sentence? What punctuation marks are placed before and after his name?

Who is addressed in the third sentence? What mark is placed before her name?

The name of the person addressed is set off by a comma or commas.

Write sentences in which the following are addressed:

1. Mr. Davis
2. Grandpa Doug
3. Rover
4. Dr. Andrews
5. Nancy

Lesson 39
Composition—Interview

Ask your teacher several questions that begin with *who, what,* and *when.*

Look up the word *interview* in a dictionary. This word has several meanings. Explain them in your own words.

If you could, which famous person would you choose to interview? Write six questions, or interrogative sentences, that you would want to ask. Use the words **who, what, when, where, why,** and **how**.

Use the person's name in some of the questions, as in these examples:

Mr. Ford, what was your favorite hobby as a boy?
Which state, Mr. Ford, were you born in?

Remember that when we address a person, we use commas to separate the name from the rest of the sentence.

Lesson 40
Poem to Read Aloud

The Captain's Daughter

We were crowded in the cabin,
Not a soul would dare to sleep,
It was midnight on the waters,
And a storm was on the deep.

'Tis a fearful thing in winter
To be shattered by the blast,
And to hear the rattling trumpet
Thunder, "Cut away the mast!"

So we shuddered there in silence,
For the stoutest held his breath,
While the hungry sea was roaring,
And the breakers talked with Death.

As thus we sat in darkness,
Each one busy with his prayers,
"We are lost!" the captain shouted,
As he staggered down the stairs.

But his little daughter whispered,
As she took his icy hand,
"Isn't God upon the ocean,
Just the same as on the land?"

Then we kissed the little maiden,
And we spoke in better cheer,
And we anchored safe in harbor
When the morn was shining clear.

—JAMES T. FIELDS

Have you ever seen a ship? Describe it. This poem was written in the 1800s. Describe a sailing ship from that era.

In this poem, why were the passengers crowded in the cabin? Why would no one dare to sleep? What is meant by "the deep"?

In the second stanza, what is meant by "the blast"? by "the rattling trumpet"? What is the "mast"? What would happen if the ship had no mast?

In the third stanza, why is the sea called "hungry"? What is meant by "the breakers talked with Death"?

Why did the captain say, "We are lost"? Imagine yourself at sea and how frightened you would be. Tell about how the captain's little daughter responded.

We can make declarative sentences (that state facts) from the first stanza.

> We were crowded in the cabin.
> Not a soul would dare to sleep.
> It was midnight on the waters.
> A storm was on the deep.

What declarative sentences can you make from the third stanza? What interrogative sentence is in the fifth stanza?

» *Teacher: See answers on page 4-5 of the* Answer Key.

Lesson 41
Paragraphs

Find the word *paragraph* in a dictionary. Explain the meaning in your own words.

Read the following story aloud. How many paragraphs does it have? What is the topic or main thought in each paragraph?

The Crow and the Pitcher

In a spell of dry weather, when the birds could find very little to drink, a thirsty crow found a pitcher with a little water in it. But the pitcher was high and had a narrow neck, and no matter how he tried, the crow could not reach the water. The poor thing felt as if he must die of thirst.

Then an idea came to him. Picking up some small pebbles, he dropped them into the pitcher one by one. With each pebble the water rose a little higher until at last it was near enough so he could drink.

—*The Aesop for Children*

Now close your book and retell the story aloud.

Lesson 42
Composition—The Crow's Story

Do you remember the story "The Crow and the Pitcher" from your last lesson? You can read it again if you like.

Then copy the sentences below. Complete the story as the crow might tell it. Write your story in two paragraphs.

The Crow's Story

I am so thirsty! I've had no water to drink for a long time. If I don't find some water soon, I _____.

Lesson 43
Picture Study—Return of the Fishing Boats

What time of the day do you think it is?
Where have the boats been?
Look carefully at the picture. Then close your eyes and try to see it. Describe it.

Have you ever seen sailboats? If you have, tell something about them.

Tell a story about this picture, imagining that you are on one of the boats.

RETURN OF THE FISHING BOATS

Lesson 44
Antonyms

Do you know what an **antonym** is? Find *antonym* in a dictionary, and explain the meaning in your own words.

Say or write an antonym—a word opposite in meaning—for each of the following words. Write the words in pairs, such as:

busy—idle

large	generous
quiet	tame
heavy	honest
broad	deep
slow	

Write three sentences, each containing one of the above words and its antonym.

» *Teacher: See answers on page 4-6 of the* Answer Key.

Lesson 45
Composition—Dialogue

A grasshopper that loves to sing and dance meets an ant that is storing food for winter.

Write two conversations which might take place between the two. In the fall conversation, the grasshopper urges the ant to play with him. In the winter conversation, the grasshopper goes to the ant's house begging for food.

Use this form. Why is there a comma after *morning*? (See Lesson 38.)

Fall

MR. GRASSHOPPER: Good morning, Mr. Ant.

MR. ANT: _____

MR. GRASSHOPPER: _____

(continue)

Winter

MR. ANT: Good morning, Mr. Grasshopper.

MR. GRASSHOPPER: _____

MR. ANT: _____

(continue)

Lesson 46
Poem to Memorize

If I Can Stop One Heart from Breaking

If I can stop one heart from breaking,
I shall not live in vain;
If I can ease one life the aching,
Or cool one pain,
Or help one fainting robin
Unto his nest again,
I shall not live in vain.

—Emily Dickinson

Born December 10, 1830, in Amherst, Massachusetts, Emily Dickinson grew up with one brother and one sister. As an adult, she was known as the "Woman in White" because she continually wore white clothing. She often stayed at home, but reached out to people by writing hundreds of letters containing jokes, cartoons, poems, news, and other information.

Dickinson wrote 11 poems that were published during her lifetime, but 1,775 were published after her death. Sometimes Dickinson would cleverly describe an object in a poem but not say what that object was. She was creating visual imagery so the reader could guess what the object was. When one such poem was printed, the editor labeled it with the title "The Snake." How unsatisfying it is to be told the answer to a riddle before the riddle is ever told! Could this have been one reason Dickinson had so few poems published while she was alive?

Emily Dickinson did help others in need. She published some of her poems to raise money for Union soldiers' medical expenses, and she spent 30 years caring for her bedridden mother.

1. The speaker of this poem notices that people are sometimes sad. Can you think of some things that might bring heartbreak or pain?
2. What does the speaker notice about animals?
3. Does the speaker want to help, or does she ignore others' pain?
4. What does it mean not to live in vain?
5. How can one live a life of purpose?

» *Teacher: See answers on page 4-6 of the* Answer Key.

Begin to copy and memorize "If I Can Stop One Heart from Breaking."

Lesson 47
Copywork

Finish memorizing and copying the poem "If I Can Stop One Heart from Breaking."

Optional: Draw an illustration for the poem.

Lesson 48
Composition—Helen Keller

On June 27, 1880, a baby girl named Helen Keller was born. The baby was pretty and bright, but when she was 18 months old, she had a dreadful illness which left her both blind and deaf. She was very sad and lonely, for she could neither see nor hear nor talk.

When Helen was six, a wonderful teacher came who began to spell words into Helen's hand. The child imitated the signs, but for some time she did not know that her teacher was trying to talk to her. When at last she understood that she could communicate with people, she was greatly excited. Every day she learned the names of new things, and in a short time she could spell out whole sentences on her fingers. By placing her fingers upon the lips and throat of her teacher, she even learned to speak aloud.

Helen Keller's progress was rapid, and after completing high school studies, she went to college. She graduated from Radcliffe College. With the help of friends, she published her autobiography, *The Story of My Life*. She overcame great difficulties, showing the world how to be happy and useful.

Why is Helen Keller's teacher called "wonderful"?
What is the *central thought* in each paragraph?

Can you find in this lesson a word which is divided at the end of a line? What mark shows that the word is continued on the next line?

A **hyphen** (-) is used at the end of a line to connect the syllables of a divided word. Words should be divided between syllables.

Find the following verbs in a dictionary: *communicate, imitate, graduated*. The dictionary will show you the correct places to divide words. Write the words using a hyphen to show where you could divide them.

Close your book and write the story of Helen Keller. Include three main topics:

Helen as a baby
Helen at age six
Helen as an adult

Lesson 49
Letter Writing

South Boston, Mass.
March 1, 1890

Dear Kind Poet,

I have thought of you many times since that bright Sunday when I told you good-bye. I am sorry that you have no little children to play with you; but I think you are very happy with your books and your many, many friends.

On Washington's birthday a great many people came here to see the blind children. I read for them from your poems, and showed them some beautiful shells which came from a little island near Palos.

I am reading a very sad story called "Little Jakey." Jakey was the sweetest little fellow you can imagine, but he was poor and blind. I used to think, when I was small and before I could read, that everybody was always happy, and at first it made me very sad to know about pain and great sorrow; but now I know that we could never learn to be brave and patient if there were only joy in the world.

I am studying about insects in zoology, and I have learned many things about butterflies. They do not make honey for us like the bees, but many of them are as beautiful as the flowers they light upon, and they always delight the hearts of little children. They live a lovely life flitting from flower to flower, sipping the drops of honeydew, without a thought for the morrow. They are just like boys and girls who run away to the woods and fields to gather wild flowers or to wade in the ponds for fragrant lilies, happy in the bright sunshine.

Now I must tell my gentle poet good bye, for I have a letter to write home before I go to bed.

From your loving little friend,

Helen A. Keller

This letter is slightly adapted from *A Story of My Life* by Helen Keller. She wrote this letter to a famous poet, Oliver Wendell Holmes.

How old was Helen when she wrote this letter? Compare the date with the date of her birth. (See Lesson 48.)

What is the central thought of each paragraph?

To what does she compare butterflies? Being blind, how do you suppose she could gain any knowledge of such insects?

Lesson 50
Letter Writing—Thank You

December 27, 2014

Dear Aunt Julie,

    Thank you for the game you gave our family for Christmas. We have Game Night every Monday, so we'll be playing your game a lot!

    We had a huge snowstorm last week. There's snow everywhere! Annie and I have been sledding every day on the big hill in our backyard. The best part is the hot cocoa Mom makes for us when we come inside.

Your niece,

Katie

Look at the letter above. Where is the **date** written? Do you see the comma in the date? *December* is a proper noun, so it is capitalized.

The next part, called the **greeting**, begins with *Dear* and ends with a comma. Why is *Aunt* capitalized? (It is a title that is part of her name— Aunt Julie.)

The **body** is the main part of a letter. The body in this letter has two paragraphs. Do you see how the beginning of a paragraph is indented?

The closing is usually *Love* or *Sincerely* or something similar. The letter is finished with the writer's name or signature.

Can you point to the date? the greeting? the body? the closing? the writer's name?

Use the above letter as a model. Write a thank-you letter to someone. In the first paragraph, thank the person and include something interesting about the gift. In the second paragraph, write about something you've recently done. Today you will write your rough draft. In the next lesson you will edit it, write your final version, and mail the letter.

Lesson 51

Letter Writing—Thank You

» *Teacher: You will need several envelopes for today's lesson. Today's task will be simpler if the teacher addresses an envelope as a sample for students to copy.*

Let's look at the example below. The **return address** is in the top left corner. Where is the **mailing address** (for the person you are writing)?

My Name
Address
City, State Zip Code

Aunt Julie Smith
1702 Cardinal St.
Rolla, MO 65401

What mark of punctuation is placed after *St.*? The period indicates that *St.* is an abbreviation for *Street*. The abbreviation for *Avenue* is *Ave.*

Notice that the city name is capitalized. City names are proper nouns.

What does *MO* mean? It stands for the state of Missouri.

Where do you see a comma?

The numbers *65401* are a zip code. What is your zip code?

Write your final version of the thank-you letter from Lesson 50. I will help you check your letter. Then you will copy it in your neatest handwriting. You can even add a picture if you like. Then address your envelope. Enclose your revised thank-you letter and mail it.

Lesson 52
Dictionary and Word Usage—*Learn, Teach*

Using a dictionary, find the word *learn*. Most dictionaries will show *vb* or *v* after the word to show that it is a verb. How many different meanings are included there? (These are numbered.) Read aloud all of the meanings. Then reread the first one (number *1*) and say it in your own words.

Now find the word *teach*. How do you know it is a verb? Read aloud just the first meaning and say it in your own words.

When is it correct to use the verb *learn*?

When is it correct to use the verb *teach*?

1. Write a sentence telling what birds teach their young.
2. Write a sentence telling what Helen Keller learned from her teacher.
3. Write a sentence telling something you have learned outside of school.
4. Write a sentence telling about what you teach a dog or other pet to do. (You can use your imagination.)

   » *Teacher: Also teach students how to use the guide words at the top of each page in a dictionary.*

Lesson 53
Poem to Read Aloud

Little by Little

"Little by little," an acorn said,
As it slowly sank in its mossy bed,
"I am improving every day,
Hidden deep in the earth away."

Little by little each day it grew;
Little by little it sipped the dew;
Downward it sent out a threadlike root;
Up in the air sprung a tiny shoot.

Day after day, and year after year,
Little by little the leaves appear;
And the slender branches spread far and wide,
Till the mighty oak is the forest's pride.

"Little by little," said a thoughtful boy,
"Moment by moment, I'll well employ,
Learning a little every day,
And not spending all my time in play.
And still this rule in my mind shall dwell:
'Whatever I do, I will do it well.'

"Little by little, I'll learn to know
The treasured wisdom of long ago;
And one of these days, perhaps, we'll see
That the world will be the better for me."

Find pairs of rhyming words.

Retell in your own words the first three stanzas. What message do you think the author is trying to communicate in this part of the poem?

Retell in your own words the last two stanzas. What message do you think the author is trying to communicate?

Lesson 54
Composition—Description of an Animal

Pick one of the following animals:

tiger	dog
bear	wolf
cat	fox
rabbit	giraffe
squirrel	elephant

Imagine that you are writing to someone who has never seen this animal. Write a description of the animal that includes the following:

why you like this animal

size

color

body covering (fur, feathers, etc.)

food

other interesting facts

Lesson 55
Oral Composition—The Farmer

Tell the work of the farmer in each season:

in spring   in autumn

in summer   in winter

Notice that the names of the seasons do not begin with capital letters.

Additional questions you might discuss:

1. What implements does the farmer use in his work?
2. How have modern inventions lightened the work of the farmer?
3. In what ways does the success of his work depend upon nature?
4. What kinds of crops are raised on farms in your section of the country?

» *Teacher: See answers on page 4-6 of the* Answer Key. *If students are very unfamiliar with farming, you might read the answers aloud and then have students retell what they remember.*

Lesson 56
Picture Study—The Gleaners

The Gleaners was painted by Jean François Millet, an artist who loved the peasant people of France. Born in France in 1814 to peasant farmers, Millet spent his early years working the land. Priests taught him Latin and authors of his time. At 19, Millet learned how to paint portraits. He was so talented the artists with whom he studied felt they could teach him little.

In 1849 Millet moved to Barbizon where he joined the Barbizon school of painters in rural France. The Barbizon school was a movement toward Realism, focusing on loose brushstrokes and softness of form. Millet often painted peasants working, depicting them with gleaming light. These paintings showed his humanity toward them. He considered *Harvesters Resting* (Ruth and Boaz) his most important painting. Millet and his wife Catherine had nine children.

The picture shows a broad wheat field where there has been a plentiful harvest. Three women have come to the field to *glean*, or pick up the stray pieces of wheat that the reapers have left. The artist tried to portray the poor peasant woman's life of toil and privation. Has he succeeded in his attempt?

Notice that the figures of the women seem to stand out from the page. This effect was obtained by the skillful use of light and shade. Find the places where the light is strongest and where the shade is heaviest.

Describe the background of the picture. How do the large stacks of grain and the many harvesters suggest that the owner of the field was a man of wealth? What part of the picture suggests poverty?

Jean Fançois Millet

THE GLEANERS

Lesson 57
Composition—A Fable

The Cats and the Cheese

Two cats once found a piece of cheese, and they began to quarrel about it. Both cats claimed the cheese. One cat said that she had seen it first. The other said that she had picked it up first.

As they could not agree which should have the cheese, they called in a monkey and asked him to settle the quarrel.

The monkey said he would cut the cheese into two parts, and each cat could have one part. The cats thought this a fair arrangement, so the monkey cut the cheese with a knife.

He looked at the pieces and said he thought that one was a little larger than the other, so he took a bite off one piece. Then he said the other was larger, so he took a bite from that one.

The cats begged him to stop, but the monkey refused to give them the cheese until both parts were even. He nibbled first from one piece and then from the other.

At last he said that what was left was just enough to pay him for settling the quarrel. He quickly ate all the remaining cheese and ran away.

Write this fable in dialogue form. Begin it this way:

FIRST CAT: This is my piece of cheese.
SECOND CAT: No, it is not yours. I saw it first.
FIRST CAT: _____
SECOND CAT: _____
FIRST CAT: _____
MONKEY: _____

Lesson 58
Poem to Memorize

The Planting of the Apple Tree
(excerpt)

What plant we in this apple tree?
Buds which the breath of summer days
Shall lengthen into leafy sprays;
Boughs where the thrush, with crimson breast,
Shall haunt and sing and hide her nest;
    We plant, upon the sunny lea,
A shadow for the noontide hour,
A shelter from the summer shower,
    When we plant the apple tree.

—WILLIAM CULLEN BRYANT

1. What type of seed is being planted? Why is this seed important?
2. How does the tree progress throughout the seasons and throughout its life? Find details in the poem.
3. What are leafy sprays?
4. Define *haunt*. What is haunting the tree? Why?
5. What is the significance of planting an apple tree?

» *Teacher: See answers on page 4-8 of the* Answer Key.

This is only one stanza from this nine-stanza poem. You might search the Internet to read the entire poem.

Born in a log cabin in Massachusetts in 1794, William Cullen Bryant learned the alphabet by the time he was 16 months old. He learned meter and poetry from the hymns of Isaac Watts and began composing rhymes at age 7. His first poem was published when he was 10, and his first book, *Embargo*, when he was 13. His father, a doctor, owned a huge library, and William spent his days reading classics and learning Latin and Greek. He became so skilled that he translated Homer's *Iliad* and *Odyssey* into English for his own use.

Bryant practiced law. He believed exercise was good for the mind and body, so he walked seven miles each day to his office. On one of his treks, he spotted a lone bird soaring against the horizon. It inspired him to write "To a Waterfowl." He also composed "Thanatopsis," a poem that conveys that nature lifts a person's spirits. As the poem ends, he reveals that when a person dies, he will "sleep," having happy dreams. Bryant was thus a part of the Romantic Movement in America.

Begin to memorize and copy "The Planting of the Apple Tree."

Lesson 59
Copywork

Finish memorizing and copying "The Planting of the Apple Tree."

Optional: Draw an illustration for the poem.

Lesson 60
Composition

Read once more the fable in Lesson 57.

Write a similar story about two little girls, a larger boy, and a ripe peach.
Write a story, not a dialogue.

Where did the little girls get the ripe peach?
Why did they quarrel about it?
Whom did they ask to settle the quarrel?
What did the larger boy say?
What did he do?

Lesson 61
Words That Stand for Nouns (Pronouns)

Read this sentence:

> Ryan loves Ryan's mother, and Ryan's mother loves Ryan.

This is an awkward sentence. Why? We can make it sound better by using some words that stand for *Ryan* and *mother*.

> Ryan loves his mother, and she loves him.

What word does *his* stand for? What does *she* stand for? What does *him* stand for?

Words that are used in place of nouns are called **pronouns**.

The following words are pronouns:

I, my, mine, me
you, your, yours
he, his, him, she, her, hers
we, our, ours, us
they, their, theirs, them
it, its

Rewrite these sentences, using pronouns in place of the underlined nouns.

1. Emma wrote to <u>Emma's</u> sister and to <u>Emma's</u> brother.
2. Mason put <u>Mason's</u> book on <u>Mason's</u> desk.
3. Sophia ate <u>Sophia's</u> lunch and then <u>Sophia</u> went outside.

Fill the blanks with pronouns:

1. _____ and _____ are invited to the party.
2. _____ want _____ to go fishing.
3. The girl sat in _____ chair, and then _____ read _____ book.

One of the meanings of the Latin root *pro* is "for, in place of," so *pronoun* literally means "in place of a noun."

Extra Challenge: Read Psalm 23 in your Bible and find the pronouns *I* and *he*. What words do these pronouns stand for?

Lesson 62
Picture Study—Michelangelo's David

More than five hundred years ago, Michelangelo, one of the greatest artists the world has ever known, lived in Italy. He not only painted beautiful pictures, but he also made plans for magnificent buildings and he chiseled splendid pieces of sculpture. The following story is told about one of his greatest statues:

In Florence near the gate of the city, there was a huge block of marble. Because of its great size, no sculptor or builder had tried to use it, so it had become covered with rubbish and was almost forgotten.

One day as Michelangelo was passing through the city, he saw the great block, and brushing away the dirt that almost hid it, he saw with surprise that it was of the whitest marble. As he gazed at it, he longed to change the great stone into a statue that should be more splendid than anything he had yet made.

With mallet and chisel he began to work. Weeks went by and the ground all about became covered with small pieces of marble.

Months passed, and still Michelangelo, with greatest care, cut away, bit by bit, the tiny pieces. If the mallet should slip, if the chisel should cut too deep, the statue might be ruined; but the hand of the sculptor was sure, and after eighteen months of careful, patient work, the artist laid aside his tools.

Instead of the great shapeless block, too large and too clumsy to be of use, there stood the beautiful statue of David the Shepherd Boy.

The people were delighted with the wonderful piece of work. They placed it at the main entrance to the city where it stood for centuries. The people of Florence thought that no harm could come to them while David stood at the gate.

1. Why did the block of marble mean more to Michelangelo than it did to other people?
2. What sort of mental picture do you think he had as he gazed at the block?
3. Tell the story of the making of the statue.
4. Tell what you know of David the Shepherd Boy from the Bible.

Michelangelo

DAVID

Lesson 63
Dictation—Quotation Marks

A little red hen found a grain of wheat. She said, "Who will plant this wheat?"

The rat said, "Not I."

The cat said, "Not I."

The pig said, "Not I."

"I will," said the little red hen, and she did.

Read what the hen said. These words are called a ***direct quotation***.

The marks that enclose the exact words spoken by the hen are called ***quotation marks***.

What punctuation mark separates the direct quotation from the rest of the sentence?

What kind of letter does the first word of a direct quotation begin with?

How many times are the pronouns *she* and *I* used in this story?

Write the sentences from dictation.

Lesson 64
Poem to Read Aloud

What Is Pink?

What is pink? a rose is pink
By the fountain's brink.
What is red? a poppy's red
In its barley bed.
What is blue? the sky is blue
Where the clouds float through.
What is white? a swan is white
Sailing in the light.
What is yellow? pears are yellow,
Rich and ripe and mellow.
What is green? the grass is green,
With small flowers between.
What is violet? clouds are violet
In the summer twilight.
What is orange? why, an orange,
Just an orange!

—Christina Rossetti

Christina Rossetti was born in 1830 in London. A happy child, Christina liked visiting the London Zoo, Regent's Park, and a wax museum called Madame Tussauds. She enjoyed visiting her grandfather's cottage where she spent many hours outdoors observing nature, such as flowers, trees, and weather.

Christina often played a game called *bouts rimés* during which two people race against one another writing a sonnet. She could compose a sonnet within minutes. When Christina was 17, two of her sonnets were published, making her nationally known. She continued to write many different poems: children's, devotional, ballad, fantasy, and pastoral. Her poems "In the Bleak Midwinter" and "Love Came Down at Christmas" have been set to music and turned into carols. She also composed stories, letters, and a novella.

Lesson 65
Verbs—Present Tense and Past Tense

Read aloud these sentences. The underlined words are verbs, or action words. All of the verbs are **present tense**, which means the action is happening in the present.

1. Birds <u>sing</u> in the leafy trees.
2. The artist <u>draws</u> pictures of foreign scenes.
3. The rain <u>comes</u> to the thirsty flowers.
4. We <u>see</u> ripe apples in the orchard.
5. The farmer boy <u>drives</u> the cows to pasture.
6. The author <u>writes</u> a beautiful poem.
7. The snow <u>falls</u> on the frozen ground.
8. The squirrel <u>eats</u> the sweet acorns from the oak trees.

Do you know what **past tense** is? *Past tense* means the action happened in the past. Rewrite the sentences, but change the verbs to past tense. Add one of the following phrases to each of the sentences. You may use a phrase more than once. Be sure to change the underlined word (the verb) in the sentence to show past tense.

last summer   a year ago
yesterday   last September
last week   a month ago

last Christmas   last year

» *Teacher: See answers on page 4-8 of the* Answer Key.

Lesson 66
Verbs—Future Tense

Review Lesson 65 and explain in your own words what these terms mean:

present tense
past tense

Then read aloud the sentences in Lesson 65, this time changing the sentences to future tense. Begin with a phrase such as *tomorrow* or *next year*. Use the word *will* in each sentence.

Write three sentences that use future tense, telling what you will do.

1. tonight
2. next week
3. in ten years

Lesson 67
Copywork—Quotation Marks

Review Lesson 63. Then look in any book to find sentences with quotation marks. Talk about how to correctly write quotations. Then copy four or more of those sentences.

Lesson 68
Verbs—Present, Past, Future

1. The shepherd <u>gives</u> food to the sheep.
2. He <u>knows</u> the best pasture.
3. The lambs <u>run</u> through the grass.
4. Wolves <u>steal</u> some of the lambs.
5. The shepherd <u>speaks</u> to his dog.
6. He <u>takes</u> a lamb in his arms.

Change the sentences so that they refer to the past.

Change the sentences so that they refer to the future.

Lesson 69
Letter Writing

See Lesson 50 to review the correct form for letters.

Write the following letter. Your letter should have a date, greeting, body, closing, and signature.

Your grandmother sent you money to purchase a puppy. Write a letter telling how you purchased it, what the puppy did when you brought it home, what you named it, what it is doing right now, and how you expect to train the dog.

Thank your grandmother for sending you such a fine present, and invite her to visit you.

Also include any items of interest concerning your family that your grandmother might like to know.

Extra Challenge: Once it is written, look at your letter with your teacher. Can you identify parts that are past tense? present tense? future tense?

Lesson 70
Poem to Memorize

My Gift

What can I give Him, poor as I am?
If I were a shepherd, I would bring a lamb;
If I were a Wise Man, I would do my part;
Yet what can I give Him: Give my heart.

—Christina Rossetti

Begin to copy and memorize "My Gift."

You might reread the poem and author information in Lesson 64.

Lesson 71
Copywork

Finish memorizing and copying the poem "My Gift."

Optional: Draw an illustration for the poem.

Lesson 72
Description—A Store

Write a description of a store, writing one sentence for each of the following:

1. Location and appearance of store
2. Type of products in the store (Include words in a series, using commas and the word *and*.)
3. Typical customers
4. Your opinion of the store (and why)

Lesson 73
Possessive Form—Review

1. The barefoot boy knows how the oriole's nest is hung.
2. He knows the black wasp's cunning ways.
3. He has seen the woodchuck's cell.

Whose nest is mentioned in the first sentence? To what words are the *apostrophe* (') and *s* added to show ownership or possession?

Words written in this way to show ownership are said to be in the ***possessive form***.

What words in the second and third sentences are in the possessive form?

Write sentences containing the following:

> the miller's boy
> the rich man's house
> Pharaoh's daughter

Use in sentences the possessive form of each of the following words:

man   king
bluebird   sister
squirrel

Lesson 74
Plural Possessive Form—Review

1. Butter is made from the milk of cows.
2. Butter is made from cows' milk.
3. The eggs of hens are good to eat.
4. Hens' eggs are good to eat.
5. The bees' cells are filled with honey.

Read the first sentence. Is the word *cows* singular or plural?
In the second sentence how is possession shown?
In the third sentence is the word *hens* singular or plural?
In the fourth sentence how is possession shown?
In the fifth sentence how is possession shown?

Use these plural possessives in sentences:

1. boys' voices
2. cats' feet
3. dogs' collars
4. rabbits' ears
5. butterflies' wings

Change the following to sentences with possessive forms:

1. The child listened for the music of the singers.
2. The blossoms of the apple trees are sweet.
3. The fierce roars of the lions frightened the other animals.
4. The soft light of the moonbeams fell across the floor.
5. The nest of the eagles was high up on the side of a mountain.

» *Teacher: See answers on page 4-8 of the* Answer Key.

Lesson 75
Composition

Read the following story:

The Goat and the Wolf

A goat was one day standing on the top of a steep rock, and saw a wolf passing by on the plain below. He immediately cried out to the wolf, "Mr. Wolf, I dare you to come up and fight me."

The wolf looked up and said, "Mr. Goat, it is not you, but the rock, that talks so bravely."

Where was the goat? How do you think he got up there?

What did the goat see? Can you tell some differences between a goat and a wolf?

What did the goat "cry out" to the wolf? Explain the meaning of "cry out." Tell another meaning of the word *cry*.

What did the wolf say when he heard the goat? How did he say the goat talked? What is the meaning of *bravely*?

Would the goat have "cried out" as he did if he had been on the ground? Why not?

Was it brave of him to invite the wolf up to the top of the rock to fight? Why not?

What does this fable teach?

Close this book and rewrite this fable in your own words.

Lesson 76
Poem to Read Aloud

The Wind and the Moon

Said the Wind to the Moon, "I will blow you out;
You stare
In the air
Like a ghost in a chair,
Always looking what I am about—
I hate to be watched; I'll blow you out."

The Wind blew hard, and out went the Moon.
So, deep
On a heap
Of clouds to sleep,
Down lay the Wind, and slumbered soon,
Muttering low, "I've done for that Moon."

He turned in his bed; she was there again!
On high
In the sky,
With her one ghost eye,
The Moon shone white and alive and plain.
Said the Wind, "I will blow you out again."

. . . .

He blew and he blew, and she thinned to a thread.
"One puff
More's enough
To blow her to snuff!
One good puff more where the last was bred,
And glimmer, glimmer, glum will go the thread."

He blew a great blast, and the thread was gone.
In the air
Nowhere
Was a moonbeam bare;
Far off and harmless the shy stars shone—
Sure and certain the Moon was gone!

The Wind he took to his revels once more;
On down,
In town,
Like a merry-mad clown,
He leaped and halloed with whistle and roar—
"What's that?" The glimmering thread once more!

. . . .

Slowly she grew—till she filled the night,
And shone
On her throne
In the sky alone,
A matchless, wonderful silvery light,
Radiant and lovely, the queen of the night.

Said the Wind: "What a marvel of power am I!
With my breath,
Good faith!
I blew her to death—
First blew her away right out of the sky—
Then blew her in; what strength have I!"

But the Moon she knew nothing about the affair;
For high
In the sky,
With her one white eye,
Motionless, miles above the air,
She had never heard the great Wind blare.

—GEORGE MACDONALD

Why did the wind wish to blow out the moon?

In the second stanza, what happened to the moon? Then what did the wind do?

In the third stanza, what did the wind see when he "turned in his bed"?

In the fifth stanza, what is meant by "the thread"? What happened when the wind "blew a great blast"?

Tell the story in the last three stanzas.

In the first stanza, *stare, air,* and *chair* rhyme. In the second stanza what two words rhyme with *deep*? Find words that rhyme in the other stanzas.

Imagine a house where people come to hear concerts, plays, and poetry readings. Such was the house of George MacDonald, born in Scotland in 1824. He was married over 50 years and had six sons and five daughters. Sometimes as many as 450 people would crowd into their home to enjoy the music, theater, and literature. At other times small groups of visitors gathered to talk, sing hymns, read Scripture, and pray.

George MacDonald believed that "art and the expression of creativity of spirit brought people closer to God" (www.ccel.org/ccel/macdonald). He wrote poems, fairy tales, essays, sermons, and over 50 books, including three best-selling children's books: *The Princess and the Goblins, The Princess and Curdie,* and *At the Back of the North Wind.* Some call MacDonald the Father of Modern Fantasy. After reading MacDonald's *Phantastes,* C.S. Lewis said, "I knew I had crossed a great frontier." MacDonald greatly influenced the writings of C.S. Lewis, J.R.R. Tolkien, Lewis Carroll, Madeleine L'Engle, and others.

Lesson 77
Special Words Showing Possession

(Teacher: Hold up a pencil and say, "Whose pencil is this?") What word did you use instead of my name?

What does the word *your* mean? (Belonging to you.)

Would you say, "This pencil is your?" What should you say?

Read these words aloud. Then write sentences using these words.

my	her	his	our	your	their
mine	hers	its	ours	yours	theirs

Lesson 78
Composition—A Story

Tell the fable of "The Hare and the Tortoise."

Write a similar story about two children: Madison, who learns everything easily, and Logan, who has to work hard to learn his lessons.

A prize has been offered for the pupil who spells the most words correctly. Tell how Logan won the prize.

Use direct quotations in your story.

Lesson 79
Picture Study—Elijah Taken Up to Heaven in a Chariot of Fire

In 2 Kings 2:11 we read of a chariot of fire and horses, and that Elijah "went up to heaven in a whirlwind." Even though the art on the next page is a black and white print, Gustave Doré is able to show intense emotion, powerful movement, and God's great supernatural qualities. Though Doré could not use the yellow, orange, and red colors we would expect for the fiery chariot and horses, the picture is charged with God's power.

Review the picture and information about Doré found in Lesson 33, Picture Study—The Finding of Moses.

1. What type of art is this?
2. Who are the two characters in the illustration?
3. What is Gustave Doré emphasizing with light?
4. Describe the faces of the two men. How do you think Elisha feels? Why was it important that Elisha see Elijah? (See 2 Kings 2:9-12.)
5. What is being emphasized with darkness? Why?
6. Normally gravity holds a person to the earth. Who is transporting Elijah? How does Gustave Doré show the invisible God transporting Elijah? What does this show about who God is?

» *Teacher: See answers on page 4-8 of the* Answer Key.

Doré

ELIJAH TAKEN UP TO HEAVEN IN A CHARIOT OF FIRE

Lesson 80
Correct Use of Words—*Can, May*

1. "May I help you bake bread, Mom?" asked little Jacob.
2. "You may help add flour, Jacob, but I don't think you can knead it," answered Mom.
3. "I am sure I can knead it; please, let me try," said Jacob.

Read the sentence that asks permission.

Read the part of sentence 2 that grants the desired permission.

Read the parts of sentences 2 and 3 that relate to Jacob's ability to knead.

Notice the use of *can* and *may*.

Write three sentences containing the word *may*, asking permission of your mother or teacher to do certain things.

Write three sentences containing the word *can*, asking friends about their ability to do certain things.

Lesson 81
Oral Composition

Create a story using one of the following suggestions. You do not need to write your story, but you should make a short list of phrases to remind you of your story's sequence. Use the list to tell your story to your teacher.

1. One day Evan met an old lady who was carrying a heavy basket. He _____.
2. One morning when James came downstairs, he found the kitchen full of smoke. He _____.
3. Jody received a dog for a birthday present. She _____.
4. Near the foot of a high hill was a thick undergrowth of brush where a mother rabbit had made her home. Every evening _____.

Lesson 82
Poem to Memorize

Don't Give Up

If you've tried and have not won,
Never stop for crying;
All that's great and good is done
Just by patient trying.

Though young birds, in flying, fall,
Still their wings grow stronger;
And the next time they can keep
Up a little longer.

Though the sturdy oak has known
Many a blast that bowed her,
She has risen again, and grown
Loftier and prouder.

If by easy work you beat,
Who the more will prize you?
Gaining victory from defeat,
That's the test that tries you!

—PHOEBE CARY

What does this poem teach?

Explain "patient trying." What lessons in school require patient trying?

How may victory be gained from defeat? What can you learn from defeat?

If a football team is defeated, what may the players learn that will help when they play again?

If an inventor fails in his attempts, what may he learn from his failure?

Begin to copy and memorize "Don't Give Up."

Lesson 83
Copywork

Finish memorizing and copying the poem "Don't Give Up."

Optional: Draw an illustration for the poem.

Lesson 84
Words that Rhyme—Writing Poetry

Say or write words that rhyme with the following:

grow	sun
kind	hear
ground	nest
tree	high
brown	

Read the poem "Don't Give Up" in Lesson 82. Notice which lines rhyme.

Write a poem of four or more lines, making the first line rhyme with the second, and the third with the fourth.

Write about a windy day, Christmas, football, a kitten, or another subject of your choosing.

Lesson 85
Contractions

What does *you've* mean in the poem in Lesson 82?
Write the two words for which *you've* stands. What letters have been omitted?

The mark showing that a letter or letters have been omitted is called an **apostrophe**.

You've is a **contraction**.

Find another contraction in the fourth stanza of the poem. For what words does it stand?

Write these contractions and the words for which they stand:

I'm	he's	don't
they'll	it's	couldn't
we'll	they're	wouldn't
you've	can't	

Write sentences containing five of these contractions.

Lesson 86

Composition—Sentence Combining

Combine into a single sentence each of the following groups of statements:

1. The boy reads.
   He reads books.
   The books are interesting.

2. The toddler draws with crayons.
   The crayons are red and black.

3. My grandpa has a watch.
   It is heavy.
   It is a gold watch.

4. Mary was little.
   She had a lamb.
   The lamb was black and white.

5. The bird is early.
   It catches the worm.
   The worm is big.

6. The student was diligent.
   He wrote a composition.
   It was long.

   » *Teacher: See answers on page 4-9 of the* Answer Key.

Lesson 87
Narration—A Clever Slave

A long time ago there lived a poor slave whose name was Aesop. He was a small man with a large head and long arms. His face was white and very homely. His large eyes were bright and snappy.

When Aesop was about twenty years old, his master lost a great deal of money and was obliged to sell his slaves. To do this, he had to take them to a large city where there was a slave market.

The city was far away, and the slaves had to walk the whole distance. A number of bundles were made up for them to carry. Some of these bundles contained the things they would need on the road, some contained clothing, and some contained goods which the master would sell in the city.

"Choose your bundles, boys," said the master. "There is one for each of you."

Aesop at once chose the largest one. The other slaves laughed and said he was foolish. But he threw it upon his shoulders and seemed well satisfied.

The next day, the laugh was the other way, for the bundle which he had chosen had contained the food for the whole party. After all had eaten three meals from it, it was much lighter. And before the end of the journey, Aesop had nothing to carry while the other slaves were groaning under their heavy loads.

"Aesop is a wise fellow," said his master. "The man who buys him must pay a high price."

—JAMES BALDWIN, *Fifty Famous People*

Retell the story, either orally or in writing.

Lesson 88
Poem to Read Aloud

The Tree

The Tree's early leaf-buds were bursting their brown;
"Shall I take them away?" said the Frost, sweeping down.
 "No, leave them alone
 "Till the blossoms have grown,"
Prayed the Tree, while he trembled from rootlet to crown.

The Tree bore his blossoms, and all the birds sung:
"Shall I take them away?" said the Wind, as he swung.
 "No, leave them alone
 "Till the berries have grown,"
Said the Tree, while his leaflets quivering hung.

The Tree bore his fruit in the midsummer glow;
Said the girl, "May I gather thy berries now?"
 "Yes, all thou canst see;
 "Take them; all are for thee,"
Said the Tree, while he bent down his laden boughs low.

—Björntjerne Björnson

The tree, the frost, and the wind are spoken of in this poem as if they were persons and had the power of speech. Did you notice that their names begin with capitals? When animals or objects can speak or act as if they are people, this is called **personification**.

What are leaf-buds? At what time of the year do they appear? To what danger are they exposed?

What are blossoms? To what danger are they exposed? Of what use are the blossoms? What would be the result if the wind swept them away too soon?

Tell the names of some trees that grow berries.

> » *Teacher: See answers on page 4-9 of the* Answer Key.

Lesson 89
Qualities—Sentence Combining

Think of a car. Tell one quality it has. Tell another. Another.

How would you say that it has all those qualities, using the word *car* only once?

You might say this:

> The car is old, fast, and red.

Where are commas placed? Give the rule.

Now think of a ball. Tell what it is made of. Tell its shape and whether it is hard or soft.

Make one sentence out of the following four:

> John has a ball.
> It is hard.
> It is round.
> It is plastic.

Notice where commas are used in this sentence.

> John has a hard, round, plastic ball.

Combine into a single sentence each of the following groups of statements:

1. Mr. James has a horse.
   It is strong.
   It is fast.
   It is beautiful.

2. The dog is brave.
   He is faithful.
   He is loving.

3. The cow is gentle.
   She is tame.
   She is useful.

4. Bayard Taylor saw a lion.
   It was large.
   It was fierce.
   It was powerful.

5. The tiger is fierce.
   The tiger is bold.
   The tiger is active.

6. The elephant is large.
   He is heavy.
   He is unwieldy.

7. The deer is timid.
   It is fleet.
   It is beautiful.

8. Glass is hard.
   It is brittle.
   It is transparent.

9. Rubber is tough.
   It is elastic.
   It is waterproof.

10. Mr. Davis found a piece of gold.
    The piece was big.
    It was yellow.

   » *Teacher: See answers on page 4-10 of the* Answer Key.

Lesson 90
Composition—Description of a Game

Select one of the following:

1. Write a description of the game you like to play best.
2. Draw a diagram of a baseball field.
   Write a description of the game, telling how many players there are on a side, where the different players stand, and how the game is played.
   Write three or more rules of the game.
3. Draw a diagram of a basketball court.
   Write a description of the game.
   Write two or more rules of the game.

Lesson 91
How an Action Is Performed (Adverbs)

Think of a word that tells how a man walks. Think of its opposite. Think of a word that tells how a canary sings. Think of its opposite.

Point out in the following sentences the words that tell how the action is performed. When possible, give the opposite of each.

She reads quickly.　　　　Dylan speaks loudly.
He acts rudely.　　　　　He ran swiftly.
Mary writes well.

Can you say sentences that use the following words to tell how actions are performed?

easily　　　　　wisely　　　　　well
quietly　　　　　neatly　　　　　slowly

Combine into one sentence each of the following groups of statements. The underlined words are adverbs, or words that tell how. Place the underlined adverb as near as possible to the action word (the verb). You may say or write your answers.

1. John walked down the street.
   He did so quickly.

2. The book is new.
   Edith reads it.
   She reads it diligently.

3. James held the bat.
   It was large.
   It was heavy.
   He held it <u>firmly</u>.

4. The tree was tall.
   It was smooth.
   He climbed it.
   He climbed it <u>slowly</u>.

5. The camel walks.
   He walks <u>patiently</u>.
   He walks in the desert.

   » *Teacher: See answers on page 4-10 of the* Answer Key.

Copy the following sentences, filling the blanks with adverbs, words that tell how the action is performed. Select from these words:

attentively	loudly	well
quietly	beautifully	quickly

1. Mary was riding _____ on her tricycle.
2. My sister paints _____ with watercolors.
3. She listened _____ to the story.
4. John plays _____ on the violin.
5. The dog was barking _____ at the tramp.

Lesson 92
Picture Study—Belshazzar's Feast

Light! Color! Action! These words describe the artwork of Rembrandt Harmenszoon van Rijn, born near the Rhine River (*Rijn* means "Rhine") in the Netherlands in 1606. He was one of the greatest European painters of the Dutch Golden Age, being a master of light and shadow, rich colors, and energy, activity, and emotion. The characters in his paintings appear to leap to life. Rembrandt completed 600 paintings – portraits, Bible scenes, and landscapes.

In Rembrandt's most famous painting *Night Watch*, he shows the captain and 17 militiamen in action on a huge canvas 14 feet long and 12 feet tall. Rembrandt reveals each of the men doing something different. It is as though each one is moving.

One of Rembrandt's Biblical paintings from the book of Daniel is *Belshazzar's Feast*. Belshazzar's father Nabonidus did not worship the true God, but worshipped the moon god Sin. Belshazzar's great-grandfather Nebuchadnezzar, who worshipped Marduk, destroyed Jerusalem and burned the Temple, taking many sacred gold, silver, and jeweled items.

In 539 BC Belshazzar and his father were joint rulers of Babylon. Belshazzar's father wanted him to protect the city of Babylon. Belshazzar, whose name means "master of the treasure," was not only expected to protect the city but all the treasures. However, instead of protecting, he gave a lavish feast using treasures taken from Jerusalem.

Belshazzar thought he and his city were safe, but God sees all things. Rembrandt chose to paint only a few of Belshazzar's guests so that the treasures would be noticed as an important part of the message. These treasures are well lit. But do you see how the greatest amount of light illuminates the handwriting on the wall?

Daniel was able to interpret the message on the wall: "Mene, Mene, Tekel, Upharsin." These words, which are actually verbs, are Aramaic measure names. *Mene* is the word *mina*, which means "to count." *Tekel* is a spelling of *shekel*, meaning "to weigh." *Upharsin* contains the word *Peres*, which means "half a mina," or "to divide." Daniel's interpretation was that God had numbered Belshazzar's days, had weighed Belshazzar on the scales, and his kingdom would be divided. That was Belshazzar's last night. The Medes and Persians defeated Babylon.

1. Look at the painting *Belshazzar's Feast* and notice how your eyes move.
2. How do the people in this painting feel? (Notice the body and facial clues.)
3. Who is the person in the center of the painting? How do you know who he is?
4. What do you see on the wall? What clues do you see that help you know who is writing on the wall?
5. What is the woman in red holding?

» *Teacher: See answers on page 4-10 of the* Answer Key.

Rembrandt

BELSHAZZAR'S FEAST

Lesson 93
Narration—The Boy and the Robbers

In Persia when Cyrus the Great was king, boys were taught to tell the truth. This was one of their first lessons at home and at school.

"None but a coward will tell a falsehood," said the father of young Otanes.

"Truth is beautiful. Always love it," said his mother.

When Otanes was twelve years old, his parents wished to send him to a distant city to study in a famous school. It would be a long journey and a dangerous one. So it was arranged that the boy should travel with a small company of merchants who were going to the same place. "Good-by, Otanes! Be always brave and truthful," said his father. "Farewell, my child! Love that which is beautiful. Despise that which is base," said his mother.

The little company began its long journey. Some of the men rode on camels, some on horses. They went but slowly, for the sun was hot and the way was rough.

Suddenly, towards evening, a band of robbers swooped down upon them. The merchants were not fighting men. They could do nothing but give up all their goods and money.

"Well, boy, what have you got?" asked one of the robbers, as he pulled Otanes from his horse.

"Forty pieces of gold," answered the lad.

The robber laughed. He had never heard of a boy with so much money as that.

"That is a good story," he said. "Where do you carry your gold?"

"It is in my hat, underneath the lining," answered Otanes.

"Oh, well! You can't make me believe that," said the robber; and he hurried away to rob one of the rich merchants.

At length the chief of the band called to Otanes and said, "Young fellow, have you anything worth taking?"

Otanes answered, "I have already told your men that I have forty pieces of gold in my hat. But they wouldn't believe me."

"Take off your hat," said the chief.

The boy obeyed. The chief tore out the lining and found the gold hidden beneath it.

"Why did you tell us where to find it?" he asked. "No one would have thought that a child like you had gold about him."

"If I had answered your questions differently, I should have told a lie," said Otanes; "and none but cowards tell lies."

The robber chief was struck by this answer. He thought of the number of times that he himself had been a coward. Then he said, "You are a brave boy, and you may keep your gold. Here it is. Mount your horse, and my own men will ride with you and see that you reach the end of your journey in safety."

Otanes, in time, became one of the famous men of his country. He was the advisor and friend of two of the kings who succeeded Cyrus.

—James Baldwin, *Fifty Famous People*

Retell the story, either orally or in writing.

Lesson 94
Poem to Memorize

The Love of God

The love of God is greater far
Than tongue or pen can ever tell;
It goes beyond the highest star,
And reaches to the lowest hell;
The guilty pair, bowed down with care,
God gave His Son to win;
His erring child He reconciled,
And pardoned from his sin.

Could we with ink the ocean fill,
And were the skies of parchment made,
Were every stalk on earth a quill,
And every man a scribe by trade;
To write the love of God above
Would drain the ocean dry;
Nor could the scroll contain the whole,
Though stretched from sky to sky.

Refrain:
Oh, love of God, how rich and pure!
How measureless and strong!
It shall forevermore endure—
The saints' and angels' song.

—Frederick M. Lehman

These stanzas are a portion of a hymn written in 1917.

In stanza one, who are the guilty pair? (Hint: See Genesis 3.) Tell the meaning of stanza one in your own words.

For stanza two, find *parchment* and *quill* in a dictionary. Explain their meanings. Then tell the meaning of stanza two in your own words.

Find the two possessive nouns in the refrain. Are they singular or plural?

» *Teacher: See answers on page 4-11 of the* Answer Key.

Begin to copy and memorize "The Love of God."

Lesson 95
Copywork

Finish memorizing and copying the poem "The Love of God."

Optional: Draw an illustration for the poem.

Lesson 96
Written Conversation

Imagine that Jordan has moved into the house next to yours. You are talking together. Write the conversation—Jordan asking questions about your school and neighborhood, which you answer.

Use the following form:

> **JORDAN:**   I am so glad you are going to live near me. Are you going to school Monday?
>
> **[YOUR NAME]:**   _____.

Lesson 97
Comparison

> Both Tom and Henry are tall, but I believe Henry is taller.
> There are several tall boys in the class, but Frank is the tallest.

In the first sentence how many boys are compared? What syllable is added to _tall_ to indicate the comparison?

In the second sentence, where more than two are compared, what syllable is added to _tall_?

Say sentences using the following words correctly:

heavy	tall	good	little	bad
heavier	taller	better	less	worse
heaviest	tallest	best	least	worst

Write sentences to compare things or people you are familiar with. Write a sentence for each quality listed below. For example: Grandpa is *older* than Grandma.

1. thin
2. hard
3. tough
4. wide
5. smooth
6. short
7. big

Lesson 98
Comparison

Would you say that a glass is *transparenter* than another glass? What should you say?

This glass is more transparent than that glass.

Say sentences, comparing two or more persons or objects using each of the following qualities:

| generous | rough | studious |
| patient | beautiful | juicy |

» *Teacher: See answers on page 4-11 of the* Answer Key.

When do you add *er* and *est* to compare persons or things? When do you use *more* and *most*?

When words are long, they are usually compared by using the words *more* or *most*.

beautiful, *more* beautiful, *most* beautiful

Some words are compared irregularly: for example, *good, better, best*.

Fill the blanks in each sentence, selecting the correct word from the choices given.

1. I have only a little money and she has _____.   *little, less, least*
2. Which is the _____ of the two boys?   *old, older, oldest*
3. There are many pretty pictures in the room; which do you think is the _____?   *pretty, prettier, prettiest*
4. This is a _____ apple, but that one is _____.   *good, better, best*
5. You took the _____ apple in the basket.   *large, larger, largest*
6. Sugar is _____, but honey is _____.   *sweet, sweeter, sweetest*
7. This is an amusing story, but that one is _____.   *amusing, more amusing, most amusing*
8. Today is cold, Saturday was _____, but last Friday was the _____ day of this month.   *cold, colder, coldest*
9. Which of the three babies is the _____?   *young, younger, youngest*
10. Which tree in the orchard is _____ from the road?   *far, farther, farthest*

Lesson 99
Composition—Two Squirrels

Write or tell a story about two little squirrels that lived in an old elm tree.

Include in your story some incident that might happen in the life of a squirrel.

What enemies does a squirrel have? What narrow escape might a squirrel have?

Lesson 100
Poem to Read Aloud

The Ingenious Little Old Man

A little old man of the sea
   Went out in a boat for a sail.
The water came in
Almost up to his chin,
   And he had nothing with which to bail.

But this little old man of the sea
   Just drew out his jackknife so stout,
And a hole with its blade
In the bottom he made,
   So that all of the water ran out.

—John Bennett

Do you like the poem? Why?

Which lines end in words that rhyme?

Retell the poem in your own words.

Lesson 101
Autobiography

An autobiography is an account one writes about himself. Use the following list in writing your autobiography:

Name
Birthplace and date of birth
Family
Current residence
School life
    Name of school
    Name of teacher
    Grade
    Studies
Favorite games or sports
Favorite books
Pets
Friends
Interesting or exciting events in your life
Plans for the future

Complete your first version today. You will continue this assignment tomorrow.

Lesson 102
Autobiography

Review your composition from yesterday with your teacher. Make changes as needed. Then recopy the assignment. Share your autobiography with your grandparents or an aunt or uncle.